# Stop Skin Picking

*How to Break the Habit of Skin Picking
and Effectively Cure Dermatillomania*

*First edition*

2

# Table of Contents

# 1

# Introduction

In 2006, I shaped the biggest scar on my body to this date from picking a wound compulsively until the wound was so big, that people constantly asked what had happened. Up until then, I had been skin picking for as long as I could remember, and I had several scars as a result. However, this one was the crown jewel and the embarrassment was real.

The creation of the scar was a project that went on with picking every day for about 3 months. I started by scratching a simple mosquito bite, then I picked the wound I had gotten again and again until there was no more left but a scar almost in the length of about an inch in diameter. After that there was nothing left to do but to leave it as an eternal scar on my lower right leg.

When looking back, it was a time in my life where I suffered a great deal mentally and emotionally, and it is obvious to me today that my obsessive skin picking came from emotional stress and anxiety.

*One of my scars from picking a mosquito bite – now 13 years later:*

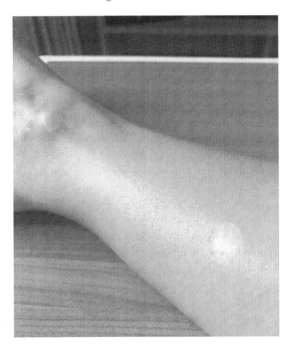

I don't consider compulsive skin picking a problem for me anymore, but it has taken time and awareness to get to this stage. I have also reached an acceptance of the scars on my body which now also serve as confirmation, that I got through those picking days and reside now in a much better place emotionally.

Today I sometimes pick my skin, mainly the occasional pimples on my face. However, the awareness I have gained of the disorder and how to deal with it effectively as well as the elimination of emotional stress makes it non-compulsive for me now.

The goal of this book is to educate my readers on the complexity of the Skin Picking Disorder and the reasons why it occurs. By the end of this book, you'll find out not just WHY you might suffer from the condition but also HOW to address it yourself or with the help of friends, family members, and a professional.

This book contains information on Skin Picking Disorder as classified under the DSM-V as well as skin picking disorder when viewed as a habit.

## Important disclaimer

By no means am I a professional within the area of Skin Picking Disorder. Everything in this book is from personal experience and research and does not serve as professional advice. Please consult a licensed professional before attempting any techniques outlined in this book.

You should always consult with a doctor or a professional therapist if you suspect that you might suffer from a disorder. You should also consult a doctor, a specialist or a professional therapist before engaging in any treatment.

No warranties of any kind are expressed or implied. I cannot make any guarantees of results nor guarantee that you will benefit from any of the advice I present in this book.

*Thanks for purchasing this book, I hope you enjoy it!*

# 2

# What Is Skin Picking and Skin Picking Disorder

Skin Picking is known by many names in the medical field some of which include dermatillomania or excoriation disorder. For the purposes of this book, we'll be using the layman's term, which is Skin Picking or Skin Picking Disorder (SPD).

So, what exactly is this condition? You've probably picked at a scab before, reopening up the wound just because you wanted to. Doing this once or twice is not the disorder contemplated by Skin Picking. Instead, the condition is characterized by repeated picking of the skin which eventually results to scratches, wounds, or lesions. What makes the condition a disorder is the fact that it becomes so uncontrolled that it lowers the quality of life of an individual.

## Studies on Skin Picking Disorder

Skin Picking is characterized as a Body Focused Repetitive Disorder. This means that you don't pick other people's skin – you pick your own. But you might feel inclined to pick other people's skin, at least I did. The condition typically appears during puberty or when a person hits 13 to 15 years of age. My problem started earlier than that though when I was around 12 years.

Both genders may have SPD although studies show that women have this condition more than men. Statistics show that between 1.4% and 5.4% of Americans have Skin Picking Disorder.[1]

Here are other facts you should know about Skin Picking according to the medical community:

---

[1] Source:
https://www.ncbi.nlm.nih.gov/pmc/articles/PMC552267 2/

- Skin picking is actually considered as a form of self-injury

- Around 4% of college students have this condition

- Skin picking in itself can be a symptom of other disorders such as Obsessive-Compulsive Disorder

- Out of the Americans suffering from SPD, 86% of those are women while the rest are men

## What Does Picking Mean?

Picking is defined as the repeated pulling of something with one's fingers. So, when you pick on your skin, you're basically pinching and pulling on it with your nails and fingers. However, picking may also be characterized by constantly scratching the surface of your skin, leading to lesions or scratches. The term picking may also encompass biting your skin repeatedly or pulling on your hair, scalp, and other body parts.

# 3

# What Are the Signs of Skin Picking Disorder?

It is often said that there's a fine line between Skin Picking Disorder and a nervous tic. The fact is that lots of people like to pull or scratch on their skin while nervous, but do not do so to the extent that they can be diagnosed with SPD. However, there are those who do this to such an extreme that there's no doubt as to the diagnosis.

If you're unsure or believe you can still enforce some control in your skin picking compulsion, you must first check out the following signs to see if you're a candidate for SPD.

- Do you pick your skin for hours during the day? Does the action take up most of your time during the day?

- Have you picked your skin so thoroughly that you managed to draw blood?

- Do you have a noticeable scar due to skin picking?

- Do you often worry about how much skin you've picked?

- Do you consciously dress up to hide the marks of skin picking?

- Do you consciously pick your skin in places that are easily hidden with clothing?

- Does picking your skin affect or get in the way of your professional and personal life?

If you answer "YES" to many of these questions, then chances are you have skin picking disorder. It's important to note that Skin Picking talks about skin in the general sense. Hence, you're not just picking on the smooth healthy skin of your arms or forearms but also:

- Pimples

- Calluses

- Lesions

- Scabs

- Scalp

- Lips

Now, there's a good chance that you're picking on body parts other than those mentioned. With the skin being the largest organ of the body, then there are lots of possibilities as targets for Skin Picking Disorder. Note though that no matter what body part that happens to be, if it falls within the general criteria of the definition, then it may be characterized as Skin Picking Disorder.

The question now is – who makes the diagnoses? The safe answer is the psychologist or the therapist. However, that should not stop you from having a hunch that you have Skin Picking Disorder and proceed on that assumption. I never had anyone diagnose me, but I don't doubt that I suffered from skin picking disorder. Later on in this book, we'll talk about Skin Picking as a bad habit versus it being an actual disorder as per the DSM-V.

As early as now, you should know that Skin Picking Disorder may coexist or is viewed as a symptom of OCD, Anxiety Disorder, and ADHD. If you feel like your symptoms go beyond that of Skin Picking Disorder, then seeking professional help is highly encouraged.

# 4

# Risks of Skin Picking

Skin Picking might seem like a harmless thing to do, but this can cause problems in the long term. Following are some of the potential risks of Skin Picking.

## Risk of Infection

Perhaps the most obvious risk of skin picking is the likelihood of infection. Remember that skin picking can occur anywhere from the scalp, the lips, healthy skin, scabs, and the nails. Skin picking means that the wound, instead of closing off and healing, remains open – increasing the likelihood of infection.

Anything and everything can come through the open wound and cause havoc such as tetanus, and staph.

When infiltrated by some kind of bacteria, the small open wound can start to fester, spiking a fever, and all sorts of symptoms. With the skin being the body's primary barrier against bacteria, an open wound makes it more difficult for your immune system to keep the body in top form.

Picking on the skin of the lips and hair can also expose the body to harsh chemicals as well as additional bacteria. Kissing with an open wound exposes your body to higher infection risks. An open wound on the scalp can also make it difficult to use certain types of products such as shampoo and hair conditioner.

Anytime you might feel inclined to pick your skin, always make sure your hands and nails are clean and thoroughly washed.

**Long Term Scars**

Another concern has to do with aesthetics. The fact is that if you keep a wound open for long periods of time or if you open many wounds on your skin – one or more of them are bound to heal into a scar. This can be quite difficult in the long run as your body bears the obvious marks. While they may be hidden by clothes, scars can still cause issues for individuals –

especially during times of intimacy and it opens up for questions about how they got there. Fortunately, scars may fade away over time – but this is a long process and requires conscious effort in order for the marks to go away.

The scar on my leg I talked about in the introduction is so big that it will never go away. With time it has faded a bit, but it's still very much visible. I use to make a joke about how it was a scar from a bullet in a shooting but eventually I had to come clean.

## Pain and Itching

There's also the fact that open wounds – even if they're small – can be quite uncomfortable. You'll be moving and the fabric of your shirt or jeans would rub against the open wound, causing pain. Itching, when it comes to open wounds, usually means that it's healing. However, if you keep on picking on your skin and opening up wounds, then you'll always be uncomfortable as parts of your body itch.

## Social Anxiety

Social Anxiety resulting from skin picking usually occurs when individuals need to dress up or socialize with others in a setting that compels them to show a little skin. It could be a pool party, a beach party, or a cocktail party with dresses that show the arms, shoulders, or a good deal part of the legs.

If you suffer from SPD, then chances are you religiously wear clothing that covers a large part of your body in order to prevent others from seeing the open wounds. Your confidence is largely affected as you constantly compare your skin to others. This can be quite debilitating and could affect your social situation.

**Coupled with Pre-Existing Health Conditions**

Another issue to note is that Skin Picking when existing with another health problem – can be a big deal. For example, if you suffer from diabetes and at the same time have problems with skin picking, then you might have open wounds for longer periods of time. People with diabetes usually have bodies that are incapable of healing wounds at the same rate as a healthy individual, thereby further increasing the chances of infection. When coupled with Skin Picking, this can cause a higher degree of unwanted repercussions.

**Healthy Skin Picking – Is There Such a Thing?**

Skin picking is classified as a form of self-injury and is generally not viewed as a healthy activity.

One may argue that the skin picked is composed of dead skin cells – perhaps the type around a wound that needs to be removed before the wound itself is covered. However, this is something that is best done by someone with a medical background. Scabs – no matter how ugly they may look – should also be left alone. Picking them off to reveal the raw skin underneath only worsens and prolongs the healing process of the body.

However, there might be exceptions to the general rule. One such exception are pimples, but not all of them. If you ask around, the general consensus is that you should leave pimples alone. Popping them would only lead to facial scarring which can be quite frustrating. However, this might not always the case. In my experience, some types of pimples heal better and faster when popped correctly. In this instance, skin picking, in so far as you're popping a pop-able pimple, could possibly be viewed as okay.

So how is this done? Later on, we'll talk about how to properly pop a pimple and in relation to this, other skin problems that may tempt you to dig out your own skin.

# 5

# Causes of Skin Picking – Why Do You Do It

It's important to first clarify the difference between "cause" and "trigger". The cause is the underlying reason for Skin Picking but the trigger can be the event or circumstance that compels you to start picking on your skin. Treatments on Skin Picking Disorder may target either cause or the trigger, depending on the circumstances. In this Chapter however, we'll tackle both of them and also discuss the possible reason why YOU, personally, do it.

## Causes of Skin Picking

The causes of skin picking are still unknown. According to DSM-V, which is a compendium of psychiatric diagnoses, SPD is a type of obsessive compulsive disorder as it produces the urge on an individual to repeat a behavior. Hence, it's not uncommon for OCD Treatment to also be used for SPD patients.

Since OCD itself is believed to be caused by genetic factors, then there's a large chance that you can also get SPD through genetics. Hence, if any of your family members have OCD, then this might be the reason for your Skin Picking tendencies.

Past trauma may also cause Skin Picking as the disorder is often viewed by most people as a coping mechanism.

## Triggers of Skin Picking

As previously mentioned, skin picking is an action that's seen as a coping mechanism by the people who do it. When exposed to stressful situations, individuals use skin picking as a way to "level" their emotions, essentially making it easier to deal with the stress-causing situation. So what triggers skin picking? It can be any of the following:

- Anxiety

- Stress

- Tiredness

- Anger

- Sadness

- Fear

Essentially, any type of excessive emotion that can be overwhelming for a sufferer can trigger Skin Picking.

**Why Do You Do It?**

As promised, this book will tackle why you do Skin Picking if such is the case. The thing is, every person is unique when it comes to SPD, so what triggers person X may not necessarily trigger person Y.

Also note that just like any other psychological disorder, Skin Picking falls on a spectrum. For example, some people with SPD pick on their skin at such rate that they only have two or three open lesions on their skin. Others, however, may pick their skin so much that their bodies are literally covered by the lesions.

Here are some questions you might want to ask yourself to find out why YOU pick your skin.

- Start by acknowledging the fact that you're picking your skin. Take a deep breath and look at the body part you're starting to pluck or pull.

- Ask yourself – why am I picking my skin? What am I feeling right now that makes me want to pick my own skin?

- Identify the emotion that's driving you. Are you sad? Mad? Anxious? Stressed? Bored?

- Once you manage to identify the emotion, the next step is to connect the emotion to an event or circumstance. What happened that caused you to feel what you're feeling right now?

- Identify the circumstance and if it can be avoided, then avoid it in the future. If it can be controlled, then control it. If it is unavoidable or uncontrollable, then you'll have to think of another coping mechanism. Coping mechanisms or substitutes to your Skin Picking tendencies are available in the next Chapters.

## Boredom Leading to Skin Picking

Have you ever seen a dog that licks itself continuously during the day for no apparent reason? Usually, the reason for this is simple boredom. The dog has nothing else to do and therefore proceeds to do something that they find most comforting.

If you are the kind of person who picks their skin for the simple reason of doing it, then solving your problem could be easier than most. Typically, this means finding a thing you can do to replace skin picking. Of course, finding that new thing can be difficult as it would depend on what you find enjoyable to do. And if you were aware of that and had no problem doing the other activity, you most likely would be doing that instead. There might be a blockage in you that causes you to not do another more engaging and fulfilling activity.

Reading, walking, watching a favorite television show, watching a movie, playing with your dog, gardening, and various other activities can be used to fill in your time so as you do not form the habit of skin picking. Do note, that you would need to engage in those other activities *mindfully* and *presently* in order to keep you from picking. Otherwise it is easy to pick while or in between you are doing something else. I am of course speaking from a lot of experience being a multitasking skin picker.

## Skin Picking Because It's There

Another common reason people pick their skin – and chances are the reason why you do it – is because the opportunity is there. This is especially true for people who pick their skin because there's a fresh pimple, a scab, dandruff, or a wound that's bothering you the whole day.

This reason for skin picking is oftentimes an act of opportunity and rarely seen as a problem by those who do it. You just do it because you can and it's there. Oftentimes, people rationalize this action by saying that it actually "helps" with the healing process – which is not the case at all. Later on in this book, we'll talk about the exception to this general rule.

# 6

# Seeing a Professional

Where you fall in the spectrum of severity when it comes to Skin Picking will determine the extent of help you'll need to break the habit. While the act is generally compulsive, there are those who, luckily, can still exercise a measure of control when performing the act.

So how do you know that it's time to see a professional?

There are currently online tests that you can take to help you assess yourself and the severity of skin picking problems you might have. Note that the test is not meant to diagnose you conclusively but rather, to serve as a guide in helping you make the best decision for yourself.

The general rule is that if the Skin Picking negatively affects your life, then it's time to see a professional. For example, you have more than one friend who comments on it which means that you do it a lot. If you also start changing the way you dress due to the lesions, then it's time to meet a professional.

If you are consciously ashamed of the presence of the lesions but still don't stop, a visit to a medical professional is recommendable. If you have big scars due to the lesions, then this is also a sign. Finally, if you pick your skin so much that there's always an open wound at any given time – then you should seek help.

There's no definitive amount of time for when a visit to a professional is needed. Skin Picking can sometimes be cyclical and thus, an individual may be picking one month and stopping the next, and then does it again the next month.

**DSM-V Diagnostic Criteria**

As per the DSM-V, there are 5 diagnostic criteria for Skin Picking Disorder. These are:

- Recurrent skin picking resulting to skin lesions

- Repeated attempts to stop the behavior

- The skin picking causes clinically significant impairment or distress

- The symptoms aren't caused by a substance, dermatological or medical condition

- The symptoms are not explained by another type of psychiatric disorder

Hence, if you meet all of these five criteria, you should definitely see a doctor for the condition. Note though that the last criteria is not exactly something you're capable of determining yourself. The doctor would be the one to make the diagnoses, taking into consideration other symptoms that might point to another psychiatric disorder.

If at all possible, I will highly recommend that you at least talk to someone you trust about your skin picking issue. It could be a parent, a friend, a partner or another family member. (A dog is not really sufficient, but could start there if you feel like it.) Together you might find out if a professional is needed. Do remember it's better to seek out a professional one time to many than too few, and in the end I will always recommend a professional if you are in the least form of doubt.

## Habitual Behavior versus BFRB

For purposes of this book, we'll introduce the concept of BFRB or what is known as Body Focused Repetitive Behavior. While Habitual Behavior can be classified as merely a mannerism, BFRB is seen as a disorder and thus requires conscious and targeted intervention or treatment of a professional.

The question now is: when do you cross the line between habitual behavior and BFRB?

Again, there's no distinct quantifiable factor. At the end of the day, body-focused behavior are categorized as problems when they happen (1) repeatedly, (2) over a long period of time, (3) resulting to adverse physical, emotional, and social circumstances.

The most important factor of these elements would be number 3 which puts into question how you FEEL about your habit. If you are ashamed of it, highly conscious of the action, and feel as though you have to hide the evidence of the habit – then you've crossed the boundary between habitual behavior and body focused repetitive behavior disorder.

## Who to Consult for Skin Picking

Skin Picking is a psychiatric disorder – which means that you'll have to consult a therapist to help you with the condition. It's usually best to find someone who has had experience with the condition and can therefore, better guide you through the healing process. Here are some guidelines on how to approach the process of choosing someone:

- First, try to figure out if you really need the therapy. If you've done all that's needed to be done in the previous chapter and nothing helps, then a therapist would be a good idea. If you feel helpless about your skin picking and feel like you cannot control yourself anymore, then don't hesitate to find a therapist that can help.

- Start your search through a psychologist locator in your area. This can be done online through the American Psychological Association Website if you are situated in the US. The beauty of launching a search through this domain is that you have a measure of assurance that the therapist you find is accredited. You can also contact your community health center or seek recommendations from a skin picking help group in your area.

- Look for someone who has the credentials necessary for your particular form of problem.

Thus, it's usually best to find a psychotherapist who managed to work with patients having skin picking problems. Find out how long they've been practicing and the year they got their license. Fortunately, license is easily verifiable online through certified organizations. Ask about where they went through their internship and their post-doctoral supervision which is a requirement before independent practice. In addition, look for someone who is a member of the APA or American Psychological Association because this organization imposes strict rules on ethics.

- Look for good rapport. This is critical because you are likely going to touch on sensitive thoughts, ideas, and experiences during your time with the therapist. Thus, you'll have to be confident and relaxed in talking to this person, otherwise you might embellish circumstances that will only lead to failure in your attempt towards treatment. This is why the first session is typically free, allowing you to properly assess the camaraderie between you and your therapist.

- Ask about the treatments they usually use. While psychotherapists adjust their treatment methods depending on the situation, there are those who are more adept with certain techniques than others. For example, hypnosis is an accepted form of treatment for skin picking but not all therapists use this method or are accredited for it. If there should come a time when you feel like you can benefit from hypnosis, it helps to know if your therapist is capable of this procedure or at the very least, would be willing to refer you to someone who is.

- Ask for the cost. While it might be awkward to ask about this, the fact is that you'll need to know how much the sessions would take a toll on your finances. Most therapists charge on a 45- minute or 50-minute sessions, depending on the needs of the client. You might also want to ask about a sliding scale fee policy. This is a payment policy that allows for variations in the fee, depending on the capacity of the patient to pay.

- Ask about insurance and their receptiveness to billing from an insurance company. If your payment is through Medicare or Medicaid insurance, then make sure to ask about those too. Most people do their search in reverse in that they first find all therapists who accept payments through their insurance company and then choose from those who are available.

# 7

# Breaking the Habit of Skin Picking – Mild Habit

Before you can break a habit, it's important to first understand exactly how it is formed. If you just noticed yourself picking your skin, then chances are you are in the early stages of forming the habit or the habit is not yet well entrenched into your life. Thus, there's a good chance that it can be stopped midway so as not to form into a full pledged disorder. In this chapter, we'll talk about habit forming and breaking your bad habits.

## Forming Habits – The Steps

According to the book of Charles Duhigg titled The Power of Habit, he discusses that forming a habit involves 3 processes known as the Habit Loop. This is how it works.

*Trigger*

The trigger is essentially the circumstance that pushes the person into performing the habit. Think of it as the thing that flips the switch, causing the light to turn on. For people with Skin Picking Disorder, the trigger is usually stress or anxiety.

*Action*

The second stage is the habit itself. This is the thing you do after the trigger flips the switch. Hence, the trigger is the stress and the reaction is skin picking. There's a cue and you respond to the cue – in the same way that actors utter a line after a cue given by another actor.

*Reward*

The Habit Loop is not completed without the reward stage. This is the reason why you do the habit in the first place – a feeling of accomplishment that you get after the fact. For people with Skin Picking, the reward is usually a sense of relief from the stress or anxiety felt by the individual.

The key to breaking the habit is therefore managing to break out of the Habit Loop. This means hitting on any part of the process, destroying either the Trigger, the Action, or the Reward so as to prevent repetition. Most of the techniques you'll find address any of these three steps. Your choice depends on which one you find most useful to your current needs.

In the previous Chapter, we talked about making a judgment call on whether the skin picking is a mild habit or a severe one that requires professional intervention. If mild, there's a chance that you can still handle the problem yourself or at the very least, require mild assistance from a professional.

**Recognize the Trigger**

As previously discussed, skin picking may be triggered by certain emotions which in themselves, are triggered by certain events. Thus, it makes sense to first recognize your triggers. What are the events that cause the condition and how do you best position yourself in such a way that it's unlikely for you to feel those emotions?

This approach stops the Habit Loop even as it begins. You'll find that there are two approaches to break the

Habit Loop from the Trigger perspective. These are (1) past and (2) present.

*Past*

This simply means addressing the problem when you're in a normal or balanced state of mind. You're not in the grip of passion and therefore can look backwards with an objective perspective. When you don't feel the compulsion to pick your skin, then take the time to study what happened when you did. What happened during those times? Remember – while the trigger may be the emotion of anxiety or stress itself, there's still a trigger that caused the trigger. You might have a huge exam coming or perhaps you failed the exam. The cause of the anxiety or stress does not form part of the Habit Loop, but it plays a big role in how you can stop he switch from flipping.

Typically, looking backwards to help with SPD is useful if the circumstances leading to your trigger are avoidable. Perhaps, you are afraid of heights, so you can avoid heights. You might be afraid of dogs which means that you can avoid dogs. If you are afraid of public speaking but find that you must do it, then you can put reinforcements to make sure you experience as little stress or anxiety as possible when the time comes. Hence, it can be argued that when contemplating past actions, you're also contemplating future ones in so far as you're using data in the past to plan future actions.

*Present*

You can recognize the trigger as it comes and act on it even as you feel it. In Cognitive Behavior Therapy – which will be discussed in a later Chapter – this is essentially a treatment procedure that you perform on the moment the negative emotion presents itself. How do you do this? Here's how:

- You feel the urge to pick on your skin. Your fingers are moving towards it but before you do, you stop! Wait! Why are you doing this? Take a deep breath and count from 20 backwards.

- Ask yourself: why am I doing this? What am I feeling right now, exactly? Are you angry, mad, sad, stressed, anxious, or in the midst of any other emotion?

- Identifying the emotion helps lead you to the next important step which is: why do I feel this way? Be introspective as you try to figure out the event or circumstance which led to this emotion. More often than not, you know exactly what triggered you into feeling this way.

- The next step is to look at the circumstance that led to your negative emotion. Understand that there are two possible reactions to an unwanted event. Either you allow yourself to give in to the negative emotion or you look at the event at a logical way. The SPD is the action connected with you giving in to the negative emotion. The goal in this treatment method is trace your steps BACK to the situation causing the trigger and then CHOOSING the other path which is a logical approach.

- Look at the circumstance at a more logical standpoint. More specifically, how do you stop it? How do you do something that will change the situation in your favor?

Now, these steps may not always work because like it or not – there are situations that are beyond your control or cannot be properly rationalized. The fact is that negative things happen and there's no way for you to control it. Fortunately, you can still address the urge to pick your skin by interrupting the second or third stage of the Habit Loop.

**Distract Yourself**

An excellent way to handle the urge to pick on your own skin is by distracting yourself. This is an interruption of the second stage of the Habit Loop which is the Action itself.

This means doing something else that will remove your attention from the skin picking and focus you on an entirely different matter. Now, the method for distracting yourself varies from one person to another, but the underlying principle is more or less the same. Following are some techniques you can use to help distract yourself:

- Drawing or writing on a piece of paper. Writing as a form of therapy also works wonderfully as it helps you delve into the reasons why you're feeling the emotions you currently feel. By writing what you think and following that path, you're able to figure out which events in the day caused your emotional outburst and from there, deal with the problem through a more rational approach.

- Drawing is a technique often used by people who suffer from self-injury tendencies. Since skin picking is a form of self-injury, then you may happily use this technique yourself. Draw on your skin using a sharpie or some other colorful pens instead of picking on it. If you see something pretty on the surface of your skin, then you are less likely to destroy it.

- Exercising is also a good way to distract yourself from skin picking and focusing on an entirely new subject that will consume your whole mind. Walking, running, jump ropes, and various other physical activities would demand all of your mental faculties, thereby preventing you from picking on your skin. It's also important to note that since exercise is a good way to get rid of the negative emotions, then doing so would help you better control yourself. Choose an exercise that you find enjoyable such as badminton, bowling, or other sports. Sometimes, simply walking around the block can do wonders to your mood, allowing you to fight off the compulsion to pick on your skin.

- You can also make good use of products today that are specifically made for people who need help with concentration. The stress ball, the fidget spinner, and the fidget cube are some of the best examples of this.

Why does this work? We'll, you have to remember that after the trigger comes the action. Your action is essentially to start picking your skin – which is an action that we're trying to solve. By walking, reading, exercising, or doing anything else to distract yourself

– you're essentially replacing the action of skin picking with the action of walking, reading, writing, or something else. What you're doing is replacing a bad habit with a new one – provided that there's still a sense of reward at the end of it. Hence, make sure to choose a good alternative to your action, such as jogging.

**Tackling the Reward**

The third stage in the Habit Loop also bears careful attention. This is the main reason or the main goal why a person engages in skin picking. Simply put, a person is anxious and starts to pick his skin – leading to a feeling or relief from anxiety. This is the reward and as long as you associate the action with the reward, then you'll never stop skin picking.

This is why it's important to cut the connection between the two. There are two ways this can be done. You can either choose an alternative action that produces the same kind of reward or you can eliminate the reward in relation to skin picking or you can do both.

For example, when you pick your skin you have this sense of relief overtake your body. However, you also get a sense of relief when you watch an episode of How I Met Your Mother or when you play with your dog.

Hence, you can easily replace skin picking with another activity and still get the reward that you crave.

For the second situation, you eliminate the reward completely. This is actually harder to do and therefore not something recommended in this book or by professionals. For the sake of discussion however, we'll set up an example for the second situation. Say you picked your skin but did not experience the reward you wanted. Instead, you felt bad, ashamed, or even more frustrated. If you're no longer getting the reward of relief from skin picking, then chances are you're not going to do it again. In the real world setting, this is often viewed as negative reinforcement and not really a good method of solving skin picking disorder.

What about the third option? The third option addresses both the action and the reward at the same time.

To illustrate: you experience anxiety and use an alternative action instead of skin picking. You promise yourself that if you manage to do this successfully, you'll treat yourself to an ice cream or you do something equally fun.

Now, there are two types of rewards that you can promise yourself, either individually or simultaneously. There's short term and long term. The short term as illustrated above is a reward that you give yourself when you manage to stop yourself from a one-time urge to pick on your skin.

However, it also helps to have a long term reward for yourself. For example, you tend to pick on the skin of your legs or your arms. As a result, you don't wear shorts, wear a bikini, or wear sleeveless shirts. Your long term reward therefore can be to buy a short dress that you like and confidently wear it after all the lesions and scars have faded away. This kind of reward system gives you something to look forward to as you move from one day to the next.

Remember that there's no reason why these two can't exist at the same time. Even as you reward yourself for small victories, you should have a big reward for a big victory.

## Gaining the Help of Loved Ones

Of course, don't forget that in order to completely beat Skin Picking, you'd want to gain the help of your community as a large. Telling your family and friends about your disorder should go a long way in helping you solve the problem. With the right community helping you every step of the way, you should find it easier to control yourself as people rally around you to offer support. More on this will be discussed on a later Chapter.

## Meditation

Meditation is often viewed as a great way to handle Skin Picking urges. Meditation is like a self-help approach to Cognitive Behavioral Therapy, giving you the chance to achieve inner peace in such a way that you won't be privy to strong emotions. Of course, meditation in itself is not as extensive or comprehensive as CBT, but it does provide individuals with excellent benefits, especially when practiced on a regular basis.

So how do you perform meditation for purposes of preventing Skin Picking Disorder? Here's what you do:

- The best way to handle SPD through meditation is through practiced breathing.

- Whenever you feel the urge to pick your skin or when you start to experience the cues leading to skin picking, close your eyes and pay careful attention to your breathing.

- Count one for each inhale and two for exhale. Repeat this until such time as you no longer feel the urge.

45

- What's important during meditation is that you allow your mind to go completely blank and focus only the rise and fall of your chest as the air moves in and out of your body. The counting helps narrow down the focus so that even your sense of hearing is obliterated by the rise and fall of your chest.

- It's usually a good idea to clasp your hands together during meditation and close your eyes. Doing this hellps your sense of touch and sight not to be distracted as you try to place your focus entirely on the present.

- Meditation takes a lot of practice to perfect, but it is strongly suggested that you try this technique for at least 3 minutes each time. Do not give up too easily because you can't expect to benefit from meditation in one go.

- Since meditation is so beneficial and something that can be easily integrated in your life, it is strongly suggested that you practice meditation on a daily basis – with or without the urge for skin picking. Try to stick to 3 minutes of meditation each day and you'll find that practice makes perfect.

- With sufficient practice, you'll be able to tap onto a peaceful state of mind at a faster rate whenever there's an urge to pick on your skin. In some instances, you'll find that you are actually more impervious to anxiety and stress if you practice meditation on a daily basis.

**Targeted Prevention**

It also helps to note which skin parts are picked on the most, so you can devise specific techniques to help prevent them from being picked. For example, you can choose to wear your hair in a complicated braid if you tend to pick on your scalp. If you pick on your lips, then you might try effectively moistening the lips and therefore prevent the skin from cracking.

In connection to this, you can also alter your wardrobe not to hide lesions but to prevent access to them. Start wearing pajamas at night so you won't be able to access your thighs and pick on them. Wear long sleeves or put your hair in a braid before going to sleep. The goal is to minimize access to these locations so that there's little chance that you will pick on them.

**Using Skin Care Products**

Of course, it's also important to use skin care products to help with the healing process of the skin. Doing this helps remind you that you're trying to take care of your skin instead of causing damage to it. If you already have scars or lesions due to skin picking, a later Chapter in this book should help you find out how to best approach skin care while suffering from Skin Picking Disorder.

# 8

# Skin Picking as a Serious Problem

While Skin Picking Disorder is something you can likely address yourself, there are instances when the severity is such that there's no way but to seek professional help for the condition. Through the help of a psychiatrist or a therapist, you'll have the option of going through multiple treatment possibilities, depending on your personal needs and preferences. Your psychiatrist or therapist should be able to evaluate you in order to figure out what would be the best system that would give you the best results.

Following are some of the SPD treatments being used by professionals today:

## Cognitive Behavior Therapy

Cognitive Behavior Therapy is by far the most effective treatment techniques used for people suffering from Body Focused Repetitive Behaviors under which Skin Picking is characterized. Also known as CBT, this is a step-by-step approach that integrates and upgrades what is the usual and logical approach to solving a bad habit, coupled with other treatment methods such as medication. Cognitive Behavior Therapy typically encompasses the following aspects to treatment, administered by a professional so as to guarantee proper guidance of the person being treated:

*Assessment Stage*

This is the first stage of CBT which simply involves assessment and understanding. If therapy was dating, then this is known as the "getting to know each other stage". Under this phase, the therapist gets to know you and up to a certain degree, you get to know your therapist. (S)he will figure out the specific triggers or circumstances which led or are leading you to skin picking.

The important thing about the assessment stage is that after getting to know each other, the therapist now helps you get to know yourself. (S)he guides you through your thought process so that you become fully aware of what's happening in the back of your mind when you find yourself having the urge to pick on your skin. Furthermore, this stage helps you establish your goals and put it into a more concrete format so that you'll have something to expect at the end of the therapy session. Other aspects of this stage include:

- Informing you about the extent of Skin Picking Disorder
- Finding out the severity of the problem as it applies to you
- Laying out the possible treatments for the condition
- Figuring out how the skin picking disorder affects your life in the practical sense

*Cognitive Stage*

During this stage, you and your therapist will further examine your thoughts, delving into the why and how of your thoughts. This is when the therapist looks into the evidence behind your thought process. This is most prevalent in people with OCD manifested through Skin Picking.

People with OCD usually have this compulsion to do something because if they don't, they think as though something bad will happen to them or to the people they love. Hence, if you have OCD manifested through skin picking, then this means that you pick your skin in the belief that if you do this, your loved ones will be safe from a particular harm.

During the Cognitive Stage, the therapist helps you figure out why you have these thoughts and the evidentiary reason for these thoughts. Simply put – is there any solid basis for your belief that your loved ones would be in danger if you don't pick on your skin right this very minute?

The second stage helps you trace the reason for this fear. Did something happen in the past which led you to this conclusion?

*Behavioral Stage*

During the behavior stage, you and your therapist assess your behavior and how it relates to your thoughts. To illustrate, you *think* that your family is in danger and thus you perform this certain behavior in order to prevent this danger from happening.

The goal is to look into these thoughts and behaviors in order to create new patterns of mindset to redirect your skin picking behavior. This is a more in-depth aspect of psychotherapy which is best explained and tackled by someone licensed for CBT.

*Skill Stage*

The next stage is the development and practice of skills to help you in real life situation. In the previous Chapter, this can be likened to treatments adopted during the Trigger or Action Stage.

Simply put, your therapist will help you develop techniques, skills, and strategies that will help you handle actual situations involving skin picking urges. This includes a step by step process on how you handle yourself from the moment you experience stress and the urge to start picking on your skin. You assimilate the CBT principles in your life so that you'll have more autonomy in controlling the urge. The role of the therapist at this point is to offer guidance, help you make corrections if you find problems with your process, and essentially give a helping hand if you find yourself devolving.

## Other Forms of Talk Therapy

Cognitive Behavior Therapy is actually a form of talk therapy where, as the name suggests, your therapist talks you through the various problems and how to best solve them by vocalizing your thoughts, feelings, and emotions. The main difference between CBT and other types of talk therapy is that while CBT tackles the here and now, other forms of talk therapy tackle the past.

For example, while CBT may discuss the present emotions which lead to skin picking, other talk therapies will encourage you to talk about your childhood. What circumstances happened to you that leads to this particular form of stress of anxiety? Say, you suffer from obsessive compulsive disorder – what were the events in your past that caused you to develop OCD?

The choice of using talk therapy is largely dependent on your therapist, based on how he assesses the circumstances surrounding your condition. If your Skin Picking Condition can be traced to a particular event, then it might help to tackle the root event itself – allowing you to better cope or understand the main source of your anxiety. However, if the stress or anxiety resulting to Skin Picking can be derived from any stressful or anxious situation, then a CBT approach is more likely.

However, please keep in mind that the two are not exclusive. Hence, it's perfectly possible for your therapist to combine talk therapy and CBT together if the situation demands for it. Since the two tackle different aspects of the stress, they're actually compatible and will help reinforce each other.

**Hypnosis**

Skin picking being a stress-induced disorder, can be tackled with the help of relaxation and distraction techniques. This is why it's not surprising that some sufferers of the condition have tried – and succeeded – in using hypnosis to help them curb the urge to pick their skin. Thus, hypnosis is in itself used to reduce the stress of an individual.

So how does this work? Fortunately, you don't have to run to your hypnotist every time you feel an urge to pick your skin. Instead, you are taught how to self-hypnotize effectively, allowing you to go to your safe space or comfort zone on a completely mental aspect. This allows you to go to that safe space whenever you feel the urge to pick your skin.

Of course, a few sessions with a professional hypnotist is still required. The patient will be hypnotized with the hypnotist giving subliminal suggestions that are acted upon whenever you're feeling stressed. For example, the patient is given the suggestion to go to his happy place whenever he feels the urge to pick his skin. He can also be given the suggestion that whenever there's an urge, he has the option to stop and control the compulsion. His hands will feel relaxed, his heart beat slowing down, and the breathing becoming even and controlled.

Hypnosis as it stands is an inexact science and therefore, should be treated cautiously. Most therapists however are capable of doing this because it forms part of their practice and is now an accepted technique for administering treatment to psychiatric patients. Since it is a non-invasive procedure, it also doesn't hurt to try this particular method of treatment.

If you prefer to undergo hypnosis for your skin picking, it's important to note that you shouldn't just go to anyone. Following are the criteria you need to look for when choosing a hypnotist:

- Look for certification. While a person may be trained as a hypnotist, the fact is that the trainings available vary. Some trainings only take a month, a week, or even a weekend. This is not the kind of hypnotherapist you want. Instead, look for someone with certification through the State or on a National Level or something from the International Medical and Dental Hypnotherapy Association.

- Look for a previous client feedback. Fortunately, most hypnotherapists today have a site or a page that gives you a rough history of who they've treated. Look for the most recent feedbacks and the quality of those feedbacks. Don't rely on a single platform when reading reviews about a hypnotist as reviews today can be easily manipulated.
- Look for a referral. Note that therapists today also come with a certification for hypnosis so if you trust your therapist, then you can undergo hypnosis through him. However, if this is not the case then you can ask your therapist for a referral. In the same vein, you can ask people who suffer from SPD for a referral. This is always a good way to start as you'll be given firsthand information on the effectiveness of the hypnotist.
- Look for insurance. While this might seem unrelated to his skill, the fact is that you'd want a hypnotist capable of delivering protection

should there be a need. Liability insurance is the one you should look for when seeking a hypnotherapist. It also bears stressing out that it is the professionals who make the point of getting insurance while amateurs rarely think of this kind of protection for their clients.

- Look for someone who offers an initial free consultation. This makes sense since you'll have to first evaluate the competence of the hypnotist as well as the level of comfort between the two of you.

**Self-Awareness**

Self-awareness is a method that teaches you how to watch out for certain cues, internal or external, that tells you when you're about to start picking on your skin. You'll find that this is largely similar to the other techniques mentioned here but with one important difference: self-awareness techniques can help even if you're skin picking for boredom or perfection reasons. As mentioned, some people tend to pick their skin when they're bored or simply because the pimple is there staring them in the face. If your reasons for skin picking often fall within these categories, then self-awareness exercises will do a great deal to help you.

- Grab a sheet of paper and try to write down what happens to you before you actually start picking on your skin.

- Be comprehensive in what you write, taking into account what you feel, think, or do physically. For example, you might have an internal voice telling you to pick your skin or perhaps, you have a tendency to close your hands into a fist before starting to pluck and pull.

- The goal here is to write every single thing, every single sensation, every single feeling, emotional thought, emotional twitch, or physical feeling. There's a good chance that you won't be able to recall all those sensations but remember that this is an ongoing process. Hence, make sure to keep that piece of paper close and add more to it as you learn more about yourself.

- You should also write down the events or circumstances that occurred which led to you feeling those sensations. For example, did you fail an exam which led to feelings of frustration, causing you to tighten your first and then eventually pick on your skin? It helps if you write down what situations affected you enough to trigger the emotions.

- Also recall the emotions you feel when you're actually picking on your skin. Do you feel comfortable? Do you feel like your chest has expanded and that you can breathe again? Do you feel pain?

- Based on the information you managed to write, list down the predictors you feel would best serve you in the future. What are the most common things that creates the urge to start picking on your skin?

- The next step is to pay careful attention to these cues so that you can employ preventive techniques to stop the urge from evolving into action.

Self-awareness focuses on your ability to recognize the cues, but it doesn't really solve the problem of what to do after you manage to recognize the cues. This is why Self-Awareness as a Skin Picking Disorder treatment is often partnered with Habit Reversal Training.

## Habit Reversal Training

Habit Reversal Training or HRT is different from what was discussed in the Chapter titled "Breaking the Habit of Skin Picking."

To start off, HRT is a technique used for people diagnosed with BFRB or Body Focused Repetitive Behavior. Still, you'll find certain similarities with this technique versus the ones discussed in the previous Chapters.

*Definition*

In its simplest explanation, Habit Reversal Training makes use of an alternative behavior – usually one that's completely incompatible to the undesirable behavior – in order to address the one you have. For example, instead of plucking on your skin, you instead use the alternative of braiding your hair or combing it. This introduction of a desirable alternative is coupled with awareness training which teaches you to become aware of the internal changes occurring that signifies you'll start hair plucking or skin plucking pretty soon. The goal is to find out the cues you have and stop the urge even before it descends.

Since we already discussed self-awareness in this same Chapter, the only thing left to discuss would be the choice or the inception of the alternative. Here's how to proceed:

- Assuming that you already have a fairly good idea of the ticks and cues signifying that you're about to start picking, the next step is to develop a response that makes it impossible for you to pick on your skin.

- For example, instead of picking on your skin, you hold onto a fidget spinner or play with a stress ball. You can clench your fists or you can start massaging your hands. The goal is to perform an action that will completely prevent your fingers from performing the act of plucking.

- The question is – how do you choose which action to use? This is where things get interesting because when people pick on their skin, it's usually a response to a negative emotion. For example, you're frustrated and picking on your skin helps alleviate the frustration. What you should aim for therefore is an alternative action that produces roughly the same effect.

- Other requirements when choosing an alternative action would be: (1) it has to help alleviate the frustration and help you relax; (2) it must not cause you pain and (3) it must be socially acceptable. Hence, if you're going to start punching the wall instead of picking on your skin, then you're not exactly solving the problem.

- Once you've determined your alternative action, the next step is to implement it every time you feel frustration leading to skin picking. Each time you notice the presence of the cues that signifies skin picking, perform the alternative actions you've determined.

As the name suggests, this is the kind of treatment that intends to do away with the habit of Skin Picking. The treatment encompasses the identification of the situations that trigger skin picking and help you find ways to better cope with the situation. Habit reversal training is therefore a lot like the self-help system we've established in the previous chapter.

The beauty of this treatment is that with the help of a professional, you should have an easier time of it as a professional will guide you through the steps. Typically, a therapist should also have a longer list of possible choices to help you deal with the stress that leads to skin picking.

Note that this treatment is specifically for HABIT. This means that if the disorder can be traced to other health issues – then your therapist would administer other treatments, with or without Habit Reversal Training.

## Stimulus Control

Stimulus control is an approach that helps you control the environment around you so as to minimize the instances of skin picking. This is largely similar to the self-help section wherein you make changes in your situation to prevent skin picking. For example, you can wear long sleeved shits, bank aids, or rubber bands to help prevent the urge from picking your skin. You can also try applying lotion on your skin, covering mirrors to avoid seeing the lesions, and essentially finding blocks that will stop the urge.

## Stress Release Techniques

This has been discussed in the previous chapter but deserves further explanation in this one. The fact is that stress relief techniques vary from one person to the next for the simple reason that stress relief means performing tasks that we enjoy. Since people enjoy different things, you'll have to create stress release techniques that will make you feel happy.

One good advice when developing stress relief techniques to prevent skin picking is this: don't rely on just one. It's typically better to have more than one, arranged at a hierarchy which allows you to have alternatives if and when the stress-release technique is not available.

Here's a stress relief technique used narrated by a person who suffers from NSSI or non-suicidal self-injury:

- Whenever I feel the need to injure myself, I start by walking around the house and distracting myself by caring for the plants.
- If I'm not at home and I feel the urge, I would usually take out the lotion in my bag and apply it thoroughly in my hands.
- If walking around doesn't help, I would take the jump rope and do 50 rounds non-stop
- If I still don't get relief from the jump ropes, then I'll turn on my favorite audio book and listen to it while tidying up the house
- If I'm not at home and I still have the urge after putting lotion on my hands, I often go out for a walk, often on some pretext
- If I can't move out, then I practice meditation through muscle relaxation. This means locking

the muscles of my foot and then slowly releasing the pressure.
- If I still have a hard time fighting off the urge, I message some of my friends who can help and know about my problem

Again, your methods for dealing with stress relief may be completely different from the stress relief techniques mentioned in here. You can create your own or follow this patient's pattern, depending on your personal preferences. The important thing is that you have alternatives if one or two fails in keeping your emotional levels normal.

## Medication

Medication is not often prescribed for someone with skin picking disorder because so far, there has been no FDA-approved drug that corresponds with the symptoms of SPD. Some doctors however tend to prescribe SSRIs or selective serotonin reuptake inhibitors to help control some of the urges. SSRIs are actually anti-depressants which means that they're meant to help with impulse control and reduce the obsessive urge to pick your skin. If the SPD co-exists with other psychiatric problems, then your therapist is more likely to prescribe medicine with the co-existing psychiatric problem.

Today, some medications are being tested to see if they can offer a salutation to SPD, such as lamictal and n-acetyl cysteine.

## Extending the Skills to Real World Setting

When you practice any of the treatments mentioned here, it's usually a safe bet that you do them in the comfort of the doctor's office or your own home. While you may have mastered Habit Reversal Techniques or distraction techniques in the safety of your own space, it's necessary to practice them while you're in the midst of a social setting. This is the only way you can truly test the effectiveness of your approach.

So how exactly do you do this? This is where the help of friends and family members come in. You can have someone looking out for you during social situations as you practice your new control techniques. Look for someone you trust who can help guide you out of a difficult situation in the event that you fail.

# 9

# Dealing with Specific Skin Picking Compulsion

As previously talked about, some people may pick on their specific body parts for the simple reason that it's there or that they're bored. While you may not be the type who picks on your healthy skin, chances are you're still picking on your dermis – just the ones that call out to you like a buzzing fly. In this chapter, we'll talk about specific skin picking compulsions and how to deal with them at a more targeted manner.

# Pimples

Pimples are a favorite for most – especially teenagers. In fact, skin picking which usually presents itself during the prepubescent years, maybe triggered when preteens start getting pimples. In an effort to remove them, teens pop these pimples and can't seem to stop working on them in an effort to get rid of the red marks completely.

The general rule in pimple popping is that you should not do it. In fact, pimples are better left alone because the body has this complete system of getting rid of it in a way that completely prevents scarring.

The exception however are pustules. Cysts and nodules on the other hand should be left alone.

What's the difference? Cysts and nodules are hard red bumps underneath the skin. They look as if there's a hard stone underneath your skin, causing an angry red bump to materialize on the surface. They should never be touched and if you're impatient for them to go away, the only solution would be a dermatologist. A dermatologist can inject something on the pimple, so the swelling will go down.

Pustules on the other hand, can be popped at home. Pustules go by the colloquial term zit and are typically red, inflamed, and having a white filled center. The center contains pus which are dead white blood cells. They're there to help with the infection but somehow got stuck and failed to solve the problem.

So how do you deal with a pustule? Here's a step by step process on how to properly pick on pustule type pimples:

- Wash your hands first. It's important to keep things sterile so that you don't introduce bacteria into the open wound. Use alcohol after washing your hands.
- Likewise, use rubbing alcohol on the pustule to disinfect the surface
- Using your fingers, gently press on the area at the base of the pustule. The goal is to exert enough downward pressure to create an upward pushing pressure that will allow the white hole to break open at the surface.
- This technique helps create an even pressure that leads to an even breaking of the pustule. This is actually how dermatologists do it as it makes sure that there will be no scarring left when the pimple heals.

- If the pimple doesn't break after applying gentle pressure, stop what you're doing and leave it alone.
- If the pimple breaks however, gently wipe off the pus with a clean cotton. Don't try to pick on it anymore. Instead, buy some hydrocortisone cream from any drugstore and apply it as instructed on the label.
- Use Vaseline as well as this will prevent scabbing.

What if there are more pimples popping out? If you find yourself needing to pop one pimple after another, then you'll have to abandon the process and just see a dermatologist. If you keep popping pimples – even if done correctly – there's still a high risk of scarring.

**Comedones and Milia**

These are also skin problems with comedones better known as blackheads except larger. These blackheads can be quite tempting to pick off, especially if you can easily notice the opening on the surface. In the same way, milia or the milk-like formations near the eyes can be tempting to extricate with the use of a needle.

In either case however, it's not a good idea to pop them open. As with pustules, you can TRY removing them following the same technique. You sterilize your hands and apply pressure on the base of the comedones or milia. If this does not work, then the help of a dermatologist is needed.

## Wounds and Scabs

A lot of people find satisfaction in picking on their wounds and scabs. While doing so every now and then is not indicative of SPD, it does increase the risk of infection as well as prolong the time period of healing for the wound.

So how can you better handle this problem? The best technique to use when you feel compelled to pick on your scabs is through habit replacement. This means that instead of picking on it, you can find an alternative action that produces a similar feeling of satisfaction.

I have also found it quite effective to take a lot of precaution to make sure, I actually don't get a wound in the first place. This might sound simple, but I wasn't aware of the importance of it for a long time. Now I make sure to use remedies for mosquito bites both before and after a bite to prevent me from scratching it to create a wound. I eat healthy foods, take supplements as well as rinse my skin to minimize inpurities, pimpels etc. More about keeping your skin healthy in the next chapter.

So, what can you do when you have a scab? Instead of pulling it off, you can try applying petroleum jelly or sebo de macho on the surface. Both have the benefit of speeding up the healing process. At the same time, they minimize the chances of scarring – which means that the wound may heal completely without a single visible mark on the surface.

But what if you have an open wound that you're compelled to pick and play with? It's usually better to close it with medical bandage so as to prevent access to the area. Furthermore, bandaging the open wound minimizes the chances of bacteria getting into the surface and causing inflammation.

**Ingrown and Cuticles**

An interesting take on how to prevent yourself from picking on your nails, ingrown, and cuticles is through manicures and pedicures. As previously mentioned in this book, drawing on your skin is often a good idea instead of picking on it. This is a flip technique wherein instead of inflicting a negative act on your skin, you instead do something beautiful or pretty on the surface. People who have Non-Suicidal Self Injury often use this technique to help them cope with the urge to cut.

You'll find that manicures and pedicures produce the same effect in roughly the same way. Instead of picking on the surface of your nails, you can choose to clean it – perhaps making use of pretty colors to make it pleasant to your eyes. When you can see something pretty on your hands, there's very little chance that you'd want to destroy that by picking on it.

**Hair and Scalp**

Picking on your hair and scalp can have a huge negative impact in the long run because at some point, the scalp can be damaged to the point where hair no longer grows on the surface. So how do you handle this kind of problem?

If you're a hair or scalp picker, then the following methods should help:

- Tying your hair daily in a complicated and sturdy knot should go a long way in stopping your hands from picking on them. Even a ponytail can do wonders if you can exercise significant control in the process.

- If you pick on your scalp because of the presence of dandruff, then make a point of using shampoo that prevents the dandruff from occurring. With the dandruff gone, the compulsion to pick on your hair should be tempered.
- If you continue to pick on your hair, you can also try using a shampoo with properties that help with scalp healing. You can find these through the help of a dermatologist or even one recommended by your doctor. Shampoo with antiseptic property would, at the very least, make sure that bacteria will not enter your body through open wounds on the scalp.

# 10

# How to Keep Your Skin Healthy

As mentioned, keeping the skin healthy is one of my favorite methods to combat skin picking and it comes with many great side effects.

After making a commitment towards Skin Picking treatment, the next step is to make sure you start taking care of your skin from now on. This means not just stopping yourself from damaging it but also introducing vitamins, minerals and supplements to prevent unhealthy skin and for speedy healing. Here are some tips to keep in mind that should help you better recover from skin picking disorder.

## Foods to Avoid

Food items to avoid are essentially food items that can cause skin imperfections, allergies, or acne. It's also a good idea to avoid or limit downers or food items that can cause feelings of sadness or depression – such as alcohol.

Following are some of the worst food items to eat because they can be very damaging to the skin:

- Refined carbohydrates, which essentially talks about bread, cakes, and anything and everything containing flour or with an abundance of sugar. There are several reasons for this starting with the depletion of good bacteria in your tummy. A high-carb diet has little value nutrition-wise but they contain high amounts of sugar which bad bacteria loves. Hence, you're actually feeding the bad bacteria when you introduce carbs in your system. This can lead to rashes and yeast infection. Acne is also a possible result because the carbs promote the production of oil – clogging the pores and causing pimples to breakout everywhere.

**Foods to Eat**

So, what should you eat to help promote skin health? Here's what you should add in your diet:

- Green Tea – coffee and green tea both function as antioxidants in that they help flush out toxins from the body. They're also both diuretics which means that they make you pee multiple times during the day. The difference is that green tea has less caffeine content which can be detrimental for the skin. Hence, if given the choice between coffee and green tea, opt for green tea. Studies have also shown that green tea helps promote the production of collagen. As most people know, collagen is a type of protein that gives skin its firmness and smoothness.
- Leafy Greens – these are packed with Vitamin A which helps with skin healing and protection. In fact, you'll find that many skin care products today contain high doses of Vitamin A in the form of retinol. They can heal the skin, smooth out the fine wrinkle lines, and give you the appearance of freshness and youthfulness. When eaten regularly, they can also offer natural protection against the sun. Of course, let's not forget that leafy green vegetables are

packed with other vitamins and minerals including antioxidants which improves the overall function of your body. They contain fiber which eases digestion and makes your bowel movement more regular.

- Blueberries – packed with antioxidants, blueberries make for an excellent snack and have been known to help with stress. They're also a good source of vitamin C which helps with the prevention of winkles. Opt for fresh strawberries instead of the jam kind because the latter is already packed with sugar.

- Watermelon – this fruit is largely water instead of fiber, hydrating you fully even as you enjoy the taste. It's a summer fruit which manages to help you avoid sun burns. That's because watermelon contains lycopene which works like a sunblock on the skin. Of course, don't forget to put on some additional sun screen layers just to be sure. The cool thing is even if watermelon contains sugar, the sugar is simple in format and thus doesn't tax the kidneys as much as complex carbohydrates.

- Omega-3 Fatty Acids – these essential fatty acids are best found in fish as well as in some nuts, and seeds. They're the good type of fat in that they're clean and help keep your skin firm and fresh. They're excellent for people with acne because they're also anti-inflammatory, thus preventing outbreaks. Don't be fooled into thinking that just because they're "oil" means they'll cause overproduction of sebum. This is not the case at all. A normal diet doesn't contain nearly enough omega-3, and I highly recommend a good brand of fluid fish oil as a daily supplement.

**Drink More Water**

Chances are you're drinking more coffee and sugary drinks than is prescribed. Switch them to water or at the very least, choose to drink smoothies with less sugar content. Water is the ultimate antioxidant as it aids the body in flushing away the toxins, getting rid of the bad particles, and hydrating everything else. Hydration in particular is a necessity for skin health. The introduction of more water in your diet makes it easier for the skin to flush the toxins and maintain its elasticity and rigidity. Don't forget that the skin is the largest organ in the body. This means that it is one of the biggest beneficiaries when you eat and live a healthy lifestyle.

## Nail Grooming

Few people realize this, but skin picking is an act primarily of the nails rather than the fingers. People with SPD use their nails to pick on their scabs, pimples, scalp, and hair and so on. Hence, it's not surprising to find SPD patients having long nails. Thus, it is essential to be extra mindful of how you groom your nails. If you only take away one thing from this book, then let it be to cut your finger nails at all times, so it almost is impossible for you to pick you skin. This should minimize the chances of opening a wound even if you do pick your skin at some point.

## Exercise More

Exercise promotes sweating which in turn promotes skin health. How? Sweating naturally pushes the dirt that's clogging up your pores – which means that if you sweat often, then you'll be clearing your pores often. Note that sweating because you're standing under the sun and sweating because you worked out are two different things. The sweat you want here is the kind of sweat you get after exercising.

Exercising is also a great way release "happy"-hormones and reduce anxiety thus helping to fix not only the skin health but also assist with curing the root of the problems.

## Stop Smoking

This one feels like a no-brainer, but smoking – together with drinking alcohol – are actually one of the most aging habits one can be involved in. Smoking dries out the skin, leading to the development of wrinkles. Of course, let's not forget the fact that smoking is also associated with numerous health problems today, including cancer. Smoking is also associated with promoting anxiety and quitting again helps with both the symptoms and the root.

## Avoid External Causes

Don't forget that your skin care break or become irritated due to external causes such as insect bites, mosquito bites, sunburn, and various other possibilities. Avoid these as much as possible by using a mosquito net, staying away from the sun, or making use of a mosquito patch. Food allergies and exposure to other allergens can also cause red patches or inflammation of the skin.

If you do find yourself having these problems, then be sensible enough not to scratch onto the surface.

Instead, make use of ointments or products specifically created for the problem. Itching creams today can be bought cheaply over the counter and can provide you with the relief you want in a matter of seconds.

**Establishing a Skin Care Routine**

Taking care of your skin after suffering from Skin Picking Disorder helps put you back on track and erases signs of old abuse to your skin. Fortunately, the beauty and fashion industry has more or less perfected the skin care routine – which means that all you have to do is follow the basic requirements for a healthy skin.

So, what exactly is included in basic skin care routine? This involves the use of a cleanser, a toner, an exfoliant, and a moisturizer.

- The cleaner is applied typically twice a day – once in the morning and another one before you go to sleep. As the name suggests, this manages to get rid of the dirt stuck in the pores, allowing your skin to breathe. The dirt – when left unmoved – can fester inside the pores and eventually lead to pimples.

- Toner – the toner works by tightening the pores. Have you ever looked at the mirror and noticed what seems to be huge holes staring at you? These are your pores and the toner manages to close them down. This has the benefit of creating an even skin tone as well as preventing the possibility of more dirt getting into the surface.
- Exfoliate – exfoliating means removing the dead skin cells through the use of an abrasive but gentle product. There are exfoliating products available in the market today, but you can use a basic face towel or even some sugar to exfoliate your skin, depending on your personal preferences. Exfoliating is something that should be done only twice a week – no more. Exfoliating your skin too often can cause irritation leading to pimples and uneven skin spots.
- Moisturizer – another vital skin care routine product are moisturizers. They function by hydrating the skin while at the same time introducing vitamins and minerals through the pores. This has the effect of directly enervating the skin so that it stays smooth, elastic, and wrinkle free. Nowadays, a lot of people are using SERUMs together with moisturizers. If you have to choose between the two however,

use SERUMs because they are more concentrated and contain smaller molecules, which means that they can penetrate the skin better.

- Sun Screen – while not included in the basic list given above, sun screen is becoming increasingly important. The harsh rays of the sun are perhaps the biggest enemy of the skin – resulting to sun burns, skin damage, and dryness. Sun screen with at least SPF 15 should help prevent the harmful UV rays from hitting the surface of your skin and breaking down the skin cells.
- Lotion – so far, this skin care routine is focused primarily on keeping your face glowing and healthy. However, don't forget the rest of your body which also needs hydration. Applying lotion at least 3 or 4 times a week would go a long way in keeping the surface pliant. Ideally, lotion is placed once a day but for those who don't have time for this ritual, you can make do with 3 times a week.

Getting a body scrub at least once a week should also help exfoliate the skin from the rest of your body. Note that a body scrub need not be done through a professional. You can perform one in the luxury of your own bathroom with some scented body soap and a loofa.

## Promoting Scar Healing

Although already mentioned previously in the book, it bears repeating that you can apply products on the scars to promote their healing. For some SPD sufferers, simply seeing the marks of their old habit causes a compulsion to start all over again – which is something we're trying to avoid. This being the case, take the time to apply a scar healing ointment cream on the surface to help new skin regenerate and get rid of the imperfection.

As mentioned, you can use sebo de macho for this, which is probably the cheapest scar-treatment cream available in the market today. If you prefer faster results however, you can opt for the more expensive creams.

## Supplements That Can Help

Supplements in reference to skin health usually refer to any of the following:

- Vitamin A – found in many fruits and vegetables, particularly in carrots, Vitamin A is wonderfully good for the skin. In fact, retinol is a variant of Vitamin A which is often added into skin care products to prevent premature aging.

- Iron – this helps keep the skin looking healthy and glowing
- Omega 3 Fatty Acids – known as a wrinkle preventive as well as an anti-oxidant, more about this supplement has been discussed in the book
- Biotin – a typical ingredient in hair products, biotin can help skin healing and growth, resulting to a flowing and radiant hair and scalp
- Vitamin C – a strong antioxidant, this vitamin is not naturally occurring in the body so you'll definitely have to consume it in supplements or as part of your daily diet. Vitamin C helps with both skin and hair growth.

## Natural Remedies

Natural remedies for skin care and healing are wide and varied. You might be surprised at how most of them can be found in your kitchen. Following are great natural remedies that help promote skin healing:

- Apple Cider Vinegar – this functions as an excellent toner and helps even out the surface of the skin. Application on a daily basis helps get rid of dark spots and blackheads. When applied on pimples, they can also speed up the healing process and get rid of the inflammation overnight.
- Aloe Vera – the flesh of the aloe vera plant does wonders for the skin and hair. When applied to the hair, it helps promote the growth and thickness of the strands. In fact, aloe vera is a staple ingredient in shampoos. The same flesh can be rubbed on the skin, allowing its essence to permeate the pores. The aloe vera adds vitamins and minerals to the skin, allowing the color to even out, hydrating the surface, and essentially preventing the growth of pimples. You'll find that many face masks are aloe vera based.

**Dermatologist**

Of course, don't forget that you can always seek the help of a dermatologist to care for your skin. Keep in mind though that dermatologists are not therapists and therefore, cannot address psychiatric problems such as Skin Picking Disorder. The most that a dermatologist can do would be to help you with the healing process as well as suggest techniques and products that will prevent further damage on the skin.

# 11

# Motivation and Helping a Loved One with SPD

The stumbling block for most SPD sufferers is not the initial implementation but the ability to keep up with the program after they started. While the possibility of regressing to the bad habit is smaller for people who had professional help, the fact is that not everyone has the financial capacity to seek a psychotherapist.

So, if you decide to handle your skin picking habit yourself – how do you stay motivated? Here are some tips on how:

## Create the Habit

It's interesting to note that in order to form a habit, you have to keep at it for 21 consecutive days. If you manage that, changes are that the action becomes a habit and forms part of your life. Thus, you should impose a 21-Day Challenge to yourself by following a habit that's designed for you to love your skin instead of exposing it to abuse.

How do you create this habit and what habit exactly are you trying to create? See, skin picking is a negative action which causes damage to the skin. Your goal is the opposite – a positive action which promotes skin healing. This is why we talked about skin care in the previous chapter. The habit you're trying to build is one which improves your skin care through a routine.

Here's how:

- Make a search on skin routine. The routine mentioned in the previous chapter is as basic as it gets and you have the option of adding steps, depending on your personal circumstances.
- Write down the skin care routine you want to follow. Be as specific as possible. For example, what would you apply first and follows

afterward? What time would you apply it and how often during the day? What about skin care products that are applied on a weekly or monthly basis? Write those down too.

- If you can, create a calendar for this so you'll have an easier time following the process.
- Place the schedule on your vanity and all the products you'll need on the vanity table.
- Make a commitment to performing the routine you need to do for the next 21 days. This is when the presence of a calendar or a journal comes in handy, even a regular one. Each time you perform the skin care routine, place a big X on the date corresponding to the day.
- Doing this will help maintain your focus on the skin care routine because in the back of your mind, you don't want to break the row of X's you've created on the calendar.

**Days Since SPD**

It also helps to make a counting system that allows you to figure out how many days you've breezed through without giving in to the urge of picking your skin. Have you ever seen one of those posts which says "X Days Since Accident"? Well, you can do the same thing, but this time with skin picking. Use a whiteboard or a chalkboard and place it on a spot that you can easily see from your room. You can also take a picture of the thing and use it as your wallpaper to help remind you every time you're not at home.

**Seek Help from Trusted Friends**

Shame is a powerful emotion that stops people with SPD from seeking help from friends. While you may feel as though you can handle the problem yourself, you'll find that gaining the help of a community will make it easier for you to cope and find ways to prevent spiraling back to skin picking. Hence, if you are of the strong belief that there are people whom you can trust in your group, then take the step and tell them about your problem. You will find that with people you trust, it becomes easier to talk about the problem and more importantly, they'll be able to offer support to help you fight it off.

Good friends and family members can look out for you, especially in social situations. They can discern the cues that you're struggling with the urge to pick your skin or perhaps, offer an excuse for you to leave social situations that you find stressful.

In many cases, people hover between SPD as a bad habit and SPD as an actual disorder. Sometimes, the difference between individuals who have actual Skin

Picking Disorder and those who "only" have a sort of bad habit is the presence of friends and family members who are willing to help. Hence, if you're hovering between the two, then bringing friends into your confidence can go a long way in stopping you from developing a full pledged Skin Picking Disorder.

But how do you tell friends and family members about this? Here are some suggestions but ultimately, your approach should depend on what you find most comfortable:

- You can do it through text, email, or any other written form. You'll find that this is one of the best ways to come clean about any problems you have. This is because when done in a written format, you can easily formulate your thoughts into a more coherent one that best describes what you think or feel. The only drawback of this method is that you have lots of time to think about the act. Hence, there's a high chance that you'll back out from sending the item.
- You can also do it face to face. You can set it up during a meeting with a friend in a secure place where you are most comfortable. Think about what you're going to say to your friend and how you're going to broach the subject while the two

of you are talking. Some people prefer to start conversations like this by showing the skin lesions first and then talking about it.

## Have a Quantifiable Goal

As previously mentioned, you can adopt a 21-Day Challenge which helps you create a quantifiable goal for your Skin Picking Disorder. Having a form of measurement makes it easier for you to move from one day to the next because you can literally see or measure the improvement.

However, the quantifiable goal need not always be in a matter of days. You can also create a goal such as wearing a dress that you used to love. Perhaps rewarding yourself by going to the beach and finally wearing that bikini. You should have a goal that you can clearly see yourself doing, compelling you to work towards that beautiful image in your head.

## Don't Be Discouraged

Do not allow yourself to be discouraged if you fall off the wagon. If you must, count your victories on a daily basis so that each day is a brand-new battle. The problem with most people is that they think that if they fail once, then the rest of the days don't matter.

This is not the case. If you managed to fight the urge on Monday, Tuesday, and Wednesday but failed on Thursday, this does not mean you lose completely. Instead, this only means that you slipped – but Friday is a brand-new day to help you rectify that mistake. And remember, you managed to have three consecutive days of success!

Keep in mind that the skin heals each time you open a lesion and in the same way, you should try to start over if you fail on a specific day.

**Seek Help from a Community**

While finding help through trusted friends and family members is usually a good idea, the fact is that not everyone wants this kind of method. Most are too shy to come out in the open about their problem. Fortunately, this doesn't stop you from seeking help from others who are less close to you. In the same way that there are Alcoholics Anonymous, there are communities or associations that can help you with SPD. These communities are also composed of people suffering from the condition.

Go online and you'll find these communities, each one having their own story about SPD. The beauty of the internet is that if you search long enough, you'll find that you are not alone in your problem.

These SPD communities can help provide much needed support as well as tips and techniques on how to properly deal with the urges. Because they've also gone through what you're going through, then they'll have a more open take on the problem you're suffering from. They will happily correspond with your questions and give you the support you need. The beauty of the internet is that you can contact them easily through chats or Facebook messenger – thus allowing for instantaneous help, even if they're on the other side of the world.

**Helping Loved Ones with SPD**

So far, this book is focused on helping people with SPD cope with their problem. However, there's a good chance that you're reading this book for the purposes of helping a loved one with SPD get through this tough time. If that is the case, then this Chapter should help you specifically even as you make use of the tips and techniques already mentioned in the earlier part of the book.

So how do you help someone with SPD? Here's what you should know:

- If a person opens up to you about SPD, then know that you are someone he or she trusts. People suffering from SPD rarely open up about the disorder because they are ashamed of it. The fact is that while SPD is a legitimate problem for those who have it, a large part of the community has not yet accepted the condition as an actual disorder. Hence, most people simply give the advice of "stop yourself from doing it" or "it's all about willpower" which, while true, is far from being helpful. So far, the mainstream community has not viewed SPD seriously as it has other psychiatric disorders.
- Do not shame your friend by pointing out the fact that they're wearing too much clothing or that they have too many pimples or scarring on their body. Shaming someone with SPD is not the way to solve the problem. Remember, they're already ashamed – adding to it will only increase their anxiety, which will lead to further skin picking. While one may argue that shaming someone with SPD is a form of reverse psychology, this is rarely how the approach works for patients.
- If your friend is talking to you about their SPD, don't try to intervene too much. This is their moment to talk and for most sufferers,

someone who listens is more than enough to help alleviate the anxiety. Listening also puts you in the position of learning more about the condition instead of making deductions yourself. Note that the experience of every SPD sufferer is different, so you'd want to make sure that you get the entire story before making any other comment.

- If you think your friend suffers from SPD but they have not yet come forward about the problem, then take the time to approach the subject in a slow but firm manner. First though, show your friend that you'll be there for them at all cost and that you're willing to listen to any problem they may have. You can deliver this message through text or through messenger in a long and heartfelt message so that they can read the text over and over again until they make up their mind to tell you the truth.
- You can be a proactive friend who helps your friend maintain control over the urges. However, try not to be too pushy about it. Set up your ideas as suggestions, each time asking your friend if they'd be open to trying a new method to help them with the skin picking issue.

- Always be ready to listen to your friend if they experience any kind of stress or anxiety. This way, they have an outlet for the negative emotion instead of spilling it out their skin. You can also help you fried by devising techniques that they can use when they feel anxiety. The latter makes it possible for your friend to address negative emotions by themselves if you're not there.
- Learn as much as you can about SPD if you really want to help. There are groups or communities today that are made up of people suffering from SPD that you can join. Contrary to popular belief, these groups aren't exclusive to SPD sufferers but also to those who have loved ones suffering from SPD. By finding out as much as you can about the condition, you will be in a better position of understanding and relating to your friend.
- Be a friend enough to recognize when the problem is spiraling out of control and that there's a need for professional input. People who are too close to the problem rarely realize the extent of it and therefore fool themselves into thinking that the problem is still manageable. You should know better and if you think that your friend will benefit more from a professional, then gently suggest this option.

Of course, those are just some of the things you can try out if a friend or a family member suffers from Skin Picking Disorder. Keep in mind that people are complex creatures and your approach would depend largely on the personality of your friend. Adjust as needed and always make room for compassion and understanding.

# 12

# Final Notes

I'd like to thank you and congratulate you for transiting my lines from start to finish.

I hope this book was able to help you to understand Skin Picking Disorder and identifying the distinction between it being a bad habit or a serious disorder. In the same way, I hope this book was able to help you handle stress and anxiety in a healthier manner, redirecting your bad habits into good ones.

The next step is to follow the suggestions, steps, and techniques provided in this book to help you overcome the urge of skin picking for good! With the help of this book, your skin should be blemish and scar free moving forward – giving you the confidence to go out into the world! I'm confident that you will now be able to stop skin picking for good.

Made in the USA
Columbia, SC
01 August 2019